Vanishing Point

Palewell Press

Vanishing Point

Poetry – Kathy Miles

Vanishing Point

First edition 2024 from Palewell Press,
www.palewellpress.co.uk

Printed and bound in the UK

ISBN 978-1-911587-83-5

A CIP catalogue record for this title is available from
the British Library.

Acknowledgements

Thanks are due to the editors of the following publications, in which some of these poems have previously appeared:

Orbis, The Lonely Crowd, Poetry Wales, Acumen, Artemis, The Clearing, Crannóg, Spelt, *wildfire words*, The Broken Spine, Dreich, Black Bough, The Dawntreader, High Window, Ink, Sweat and Tears, Gwrthryfel/Uprising; An Anthology of Radical Poetry (edited Mike Jenkins, Culture Matters) and 'Our Own Co-ordinates' (Sídhe Press)

First Snowdrop won the Shepton Mallet Snowdrop Festival Competition, February 2022
Urban Fox was joint winner of the 2022 Broken Spine Arts Collective Competition
Constellations was placed third in the Second Light Poetry Competition, 2021
Blue Hour was runner-up in the 2022 Wirral Open Poetry Competition
Woodpecker was highly commended in the 2022 Wirral Open Poetry Competition
Solastalgia (under title Alpinism) was commended in the 2023 Magma Poetry Competition
The Revenant House was one of 6 winners of the Autumn 2023 Poetry Society Members Competition
Dreamscape was placed second in the 2023 'Love the Words' competition
The Museum of Past Culture won the 2023 Second Light Competition (Long Poem category)

My grateful thanks to the members of SA Stanza, the Poetry Matters Collective, Penfro Poets and Lampeter Writers for their wise and constructive feedback on many of the poems.

Dedication

For John Howard Reed, 1947 – 2023

With love and special thanks to David and Joan Nicholson, Sue Moules, Pamela Petro, Menna Elfyn and the many other friends who have supported me through a very difficult time.

Contents

Vanish

Some days the land is stolen from itself,
chimneys and slate roofs swallowed, village
and pit-head lost to this cold mouth of mist

as it muffles hymn and chapel bell, silences
the scold of crows that crowd around
the plough like a flock of ranting preachers.

It snags on fence and gorse, collects in hollows,
conjures rabbits secretly from burrows. Egrets
skim the river, small ghosts on gauzy wings.

Maps are useless now, in a world of blinded
signs. Mountains pull up roots, drift away
to the vanishing point like wandering erratics.

Fields' old names have gone: Cae Gwair,
Cae Gwyn, Cae Derlwyn, their winter stubble
bleached to a wash of heron-grey.

Some days it comes in so densely, it seems
the dead have returned, cluster in damp
ranks, blowsy as hooped petticoats.

Here I am a slow dissolve; a disappearing
landmark in this place, where nothing is solid
or certain, not even the quiet constancy of flesh.

First Snowdrop

A new-born's eyes might open like this, stitching
themselves to the light, a surprise of wind

on petals delicate as pupils. Learning to root
in sun, close for dark, to winch their lantern heads

through the long slow haul of hail and bitter rain.
I planted them on my mother's grave, a clench

of dormant buds. All summer they lay beneath
the earth, breathed in her perfumed bones.

Now I draw up snowdrops from myself, to flourish
in the cold months. They live inside my skin,

a quiet annunciation. See how they spring
in my footsteps, how they shroud the world

in white. I reach out, touch their stems, feel
the beat of her pulse in my questing fingers.

Dreamscape

A spilled ink-pot of rooks glides
beneath my eyelids; the moon wanders

in its potting-shed of stars, runs the earth
through its fingers, hoping to catch the moment

when a seed unfurls. In sleep I hear the creaking
of the sun, rising in someone else's day,

yap of fox as he ferals the night
a scribble of shadow below the trees' graffiti.

If I wake now, I'll see how flies are drowsing
upside down, watch caterpillars shift and bristle,

wrapped in their tight cocoons; spiders work
their spinning-wheels, geometries of grass and stem.

Dawn cracks its yolk across the sky. I stir from
unremembered dreams. Worlds fly from my tongue.

Fox

just out of cubhood
and taken before her maidenhead
had been breached
I find her
slipped from herself
as if she'd flytipped her body
into the lane
eyes blown into dark glass
fur starched by rain

I remember
my grandmother's parlour
sleeping beneath its weight of dust
the polished bell jars
of small dolls
in lace-trimmed frocks
china eyes half closed

and there a fox
stuffed into life inside his cloche
standing in a landscape
of felted rocks
dried grasses at his feet
lips drawn back to show
a glimpse of pointed teeth

orange hawkbit
is bright as bonefire in the hedge
as though flesh
had woken from a dream of death
planted itself here among knapweed
and thistle to burn
its candle inside a votive jar

Underland

The fields that used to be here
are chapelled underground,

holding quiet services
below the flow of traffic.

They have learned the ways
of concrete, slip parts of themselves

through tarmac cracks; the art
of infiltration, to be unburied,

and rise again in small insinuations.
Hidden in horizons of silt and stone,

an earnest of seeds prays for the will
to stifle their need for light,

to accept the obeyance of dark;
and here, would you not wish

to stay for evensong, the psalms
of coffined roots, sermons of bones?

To our bats, dancing in moonlight

Tangle in me if you must; nothing would be
more beautiful than a headful of pipistrelles,
for your hair to click and sing; to feel wings
wrap round the temple of your brain,
a quiet roosting in the cerebellum.

Dance with me in the garden, not a waltz
or anything sedate, but the whirl of jitterbug,
beneath a moon that's seen it all before, but still
peeps round a flounce of cloud to watch
this cauldron boogie to the sound of songflight.

I will pin insects with my thumbs, let that flickering
movement find a door to the eyes; open
the chambers of my heart, so they can circle
my veins. I'll filter out the world's cacophony
under the clack and slap of a hundred castanets.

I'll be a penny-hang of bats, strung from the trees'
tall gibbet; when danger threatens, or a tempting wind
carries swarms of insects in its grip, we'll free-fall
from the branches, open our parachutes of skin to glide
across the garden. I'll learn to navigate the air by sonar,

listen to the echoes of the living and the dead;
and when I die, it will be upside down, slowly stiffening
in my liminal state, held in the arms of a sturdy oak.
I will be mourned by all the creatures of the night,
and my shroud will be a winding of leathery membranes.

Blue Hour

My mother presses clippings
into the leather album; trees, hills,
pieces of field and hedgerow fixed
firmly into place with sticky corners.
A daffodil, startled by flash into moving
at the wrong time. Old polaroids of us,
pollarded and grainy, or leaning slant
to the lens, disappearing to a vista
where sky is always out-of-focus blue.

She adds a cottage, snipped out
from her dreams. Thatched roof, roses round
the door. Time-lapse of leaves unfurling.
A garden brimming with cornflower,
lavender. She trims back scraps of larkspur,
glues them carefully into the pages.
Each sightline gives her an offcut;
glimpses of sea and snowy peaks,
sun airbrushed into distance.

In the blue hour she's surrounded
by forget-me-nots, delphiniums,
magpie wings. She's hazy in this dusk,
over-exposed by a shaky hand,
merged into sheets haloed by diffraction.
I hold her tight, try to stop her from
seeping into the dark, sharpen her
blurred edges with a click of the shutter,
bring her back to the light.

Horseshoe

It lay by the gate to the grazing-pasture, spellbound
by sun in a nest of winter grass. Such luck you need to
keep,

it won't come twice. My palm was the hoof to which
this mettle curved, as if it had been hammered into place

with a copper-coated nail. In its touch was the coldness
of lost things, the heat of the flame that made it.

I stored it in a pocket. My fingers traced the sickle-moon,
hooked themselves to imperfections; this was the shape

that harboured dreams of lottery wins, success, another
life. Perhaps it was imagination, but weight had lifted

from the day, air suddenly unshod. I thought
of the horse it had come from, if its own luck had been
shed;

of how we cling to childish rituals – jumping cracks,
hoarding
old beliefs, hanging our cast-off grief above the door.

When the Starlings Left

There's absence here. Lost voices in the trees,
the quibble of sunrise staking claim to light
and seed, pulling me early from my bed
this lingering winter. Soon swallows will return,
elegant in dark-blue tailcoats, martins busy
themselves with chores inside the eaves.
But I grieve that rising froth of noise, the way
the beech hung birds on every branch,
a chattering chandelier, its prisms of song.
Other losses, too, as the year swings round
to Spring, the clock leaps forward
and I want to turn back its hands,
see starlings perched in their usual place;
you, sitting again in your favourite chair.

Colours for the Lost

We only have the bones; imagine green
for dinosaurs, shades of prehistoric seas.

Grey for weightier creatures, ichthyosaur and mammoth;
storm clouds, charcoal, flint. The colour of worry.

Fur is problematic. Think of chestnut, cast-off leaves,
dragonfly husks on reeds; anything sere and withered.

When it comes to the birds, imagination flies
to sorbet-yellow moon, a splash of azure.

The colour of loss: bleached coral, mountain hares,
unspooling icebergs. Pale skin in alabaster sheets,
cornflowers leaching blue. Bones brittling in a desert.

Mending the Night

I'm sewing up the dark, knitting shadows
into dusky throws, darning chinks and gleams,
snuffing out the glare with patchwork blankets.

Light has opened its book of hours, gilded
the night with neon. Rain dusts grass with glitter,
uncurtained windows pave the road with gold.

Jackdaw natters in lit ginnel, street lamps bright
enough to charm his eye with glint of fallen coins.
At two am, the blackbird shouts a morning serenade.

Rabbit skull hides in a heart of gorse, fingered
by prickles, undisturbed, but bedstraw
slumbers fitfully under a blaze of sodium.

Inside a twist of ivy, a universe is waiting to be born,
five tiny moons, huddled in the nest's deep galaxy.
I wrap the evening gently round their hatching.

For them I'll deconstruct the stars, smash filament
and lantern, crochet feathers of perfect dark
so they can live and grow by their own light.

Coming Home

Sometimes a swallow, returning to his roost
will pause above these fields; take the ribbon
of road or river, wind it round his beak to guide
him home He soars in blue-wash sky, tuned to
the city's fractals, the astrolabe of stars. He learned
to fly in this place. Schooled on the thermals rising
from roof and chimney, he'd glide the line of isobars
until he'd nailed it, the art of skimming on a current,
turning in wind-shear or a sudden trough. In winter
he never forgot the contours of known hills,
shades of heather and burnt umber, gold-glint
of shining wheat; remembered that sleeping town,
pulled from the liquid furnace of the earth.
Below him now, a stride of pylons, turbines stretching
their starfish arms, haunt of unfamiliar rafters.

Fallout

rain fell differently that year
air hung on its chains
clothed in a plume of ions

it lay beneath the ground
bitter as history
or a buried tongue

some said the sheep were glowing
in the dark
ghosting fields with blue light
their hooves dusted with stars

lambs with two heads
plucked from their mothers
as preachers crossed themselves
sprinkled unholy water

larks' songs sparkled
with particles
fish were darting torches in the river

I marvel still
at the brilliance
of my wings

*The Chernobyl disaster of 1986 affected farms in North
Wales for many decades*

Shepherd

Look how the day springs up behind him,
like heather after a footstep, or a lamb
you thought dead who struggles into life
from a hard birth. From his parted lips
he seems to be praying, but he is reciting
the mantra of his flock, counting their numbers,
noting the smit marks, the crimp of the coat,
condition of each fleece. He leans on his crook;
the night has been long, he is weary,
but a man will not rest until his work is done.

The moon still lingers in this summer dawn,
as new sun rises over the horizon, fingertips
the hare in his form, hedgehogs dreaming
of worms and beetles, rabbits hunkered down
in burrows, swaddled to each other the way
clouds cling together before a thunderstorm.
Small deaths fly away on delicate wings.
The sheep call themselves awake; grass rises
to their eager mouths, as the shepherd drags himself
from sleep, listens for the comfort of his ewes.

Look how, at the end of the day, light follows
him like a faithful sheepdog, trailing its nose
along the fields and the old ways, casting his
shadow large before him, so he becomes a giant
of a man, as stark and strong before the heavens
as the hills that stretch above him. See how
his sheep dwindle with the distance – in
the darkening of the sky, they are flecks of ash
in his eyes. How the farmhouse throws its glow
like a welcome, or the answer to a prayer.

Urchin

No scruffy creature of the streets,
but an old man, prickly with his years,
shuffling round the garden at twilight.
Like my father, you say, remembering
that Saturday night stumble from the pub,
how he curled up into himself.
You could never prise him open.

My grandfather as magpie

I knew when I saw him shake rain from his coat,
that puzzled pause as he struggled to do up the buttons.

It was the arrogant manner, how wings beat the air
with a punch, and quarrels flew from the branches.

I knew when I saw my grandmother iron the creases
from his feathers, shrink away from his bluster;

how she cradled him tight, didn't flinch at the scratches.
She'd sing to him from the tree-tops and never complain,

place his tattered mind inside the nest, rescue him when
he toppled out, wipe a squirm of words from his tongue.

Iceberg

Iceberg Alley, Newfoundland

He arrives unexpectedly, rafting down
the currents, hitching a ride on the Atlantic drifts,

a hobo with his rucksack of bulky ice. He sets up
camp outside the town, grazes at the shoreline.

At night he parties wildly, bowling snowballs
over waves, perfecting strike and hook-shot

along the shipping lanes. I hear the tuning
of bassoon, deep notes of organ and tuba.

In the mornings he's hungover, sweats in
the sun, creaks like an ancient rocking-chair.

He smells of fish and polar bears. Bones of fox
and musk ox, wintering their flesh inside him.

His death is a slow ablation, his life-blood
draining down to the turbulent water.

I think of how many tears are frozen within
his heart. Enough to drown the world.

The Light Gatherers

That year we all collected light. Stuffed it into
bags and pockets, hoarded the dawn in cellars,
frightened that supplies would ebb away.

It grew profusely in a summer starved of rain,
spread buttery pools on road and hedgerow.
Spiders wove it into webs, birds built radiant nests.

Dandelion clocks were glitter-balls, rabbits fizzed
in the dark. We harvested the ripe crop, stacked
the golden sheaves, a stash to last the winter.

Mice nibbled light until their bodies shone.
Through long cold months we fed it to the cows
until they were beacons in the grey fields

and lit their own way to the milking-sheds.
The light for you was palliative, would not cure.
But we'd saved enough to keep you strong

until the following Spring, when buds threw
their shutters open again and the old light
flickered briefly, then quietly slipped away.

Oak

The leaves are slowing down, starting to detach
from the living branch. Mist wanders the riverbank,

settles in the last ploughed furrows of summer.
Underneath the soil, a snuggle of buds prepare

for winter's cold; the hare's womb rests from breeding,
her young already grown into their own new selves.

I push my fist into the bole of a memory; strong
and sturdy, it resists my rooting fingers, as owls' eyes

flicker like beacons, fungi bracket the trunk, moth wings
are a tremolo in evening air. What can hide in a tree?

A girl's heart pressed against rotting bark, still beating
its escape; squirrel's mossy drey, crevices of larvae,

the bustle of beetles and wood ants, and at the base,
a clustered bruise of nightshade. Wind batters and blusters

through swaying crowns, the world held safe inside this
sanctuary of oak, standing guard over all the season's
dead.

Misogyny and Blossom

Always anticipation for the unclenching
of a bud, as she blossoms sweetly into herself.

If she kneels to the light, it's to ask for blessing
for the fruits that swell from her ovary, pardon

for her sin of opening up to any passing insect.
A common hoar in winter, now the chastity

of quickthorn petals unfolds, a promise
of haws in their creamy flourish. Don't pluck her

before she's ready, or bring her into your house;
she is armed against you, carries the smell of death.

Wrenched from the stem, she's a frothy bouquet,
a pink-blush trophy-bloom for your buttonhole.

Her place is in a gaudy vase, bridal wildness tamed
as she wilts before the admiring gaze of strangers.

Even as wind deflowers her, she's yearning for
the sun; his burning touch, the wither of his smile.

Heron

Perched on the edge, a model posing
for a photograph. Betty Grable legs,
a ballerina neck. He should be snapped
in black-and-white to capture
the monochrome of his feathers.
He stabs, quick lunge. The chub flaps
in his beak; he grapples it to a firmer grip.
I've seen him take a frog from this river,
a small green struggle in the afternoon.

This candid air, this bearing, remind me
of my father, his gentlemanly ways
and spindly limbs. He too was precise,
careful in his habits, would gut a trout
meticulously, like a surgeon opening up
the spine. A thin incision, prising back
its earthy flesh to clean it for the pan.

In later years, his shoulders hunch.
His face now shaded with greyness,
he slowly wades from bed to chair
to bathroom, leaning on the gaff
that keeps him upright. Lips clench
together, tight with pain, as if there is
a hindrance of fish inside his gullet.

And when the time for leaving comes,
he's more fish than heron, a flail
in the mouth of something bigger than him.
But somewhere is an opening up
of wings, uncreasing from their folds
like the paper aeroplanes he made for me
that soared above the garden.

And I see that this lifting is good,
the weight gone back to earth,
how elegant he is still, though his legs
are hesitant and trail behind him.
But his wings are strong, ready to fly,
and they raise him up so powerfully
and with such grace that all I can do
is marvel, know it's right to let him go.

My mother was also a kenning

Her roots were deep in earth. Mushroom-seeker,
berry-picker, she foraged to feed a growing brood.

Sometimes it was easier to live with the dead;
burrow-snuggler, pale stealer of setts and tunnels,

she'd settle beneath the ground at night, wrap
darkness round her like an unwashed duvet;

worm-whisperer, companion of mole and badger,
leaving the world to wear its grief alone.

She was surprising, in the way underland creatures
can be, always popping out at unexpected moments

to be stuck in another Groundhog Day, where she
must repeat the cycles of washing, caring, cleaning.

My mother was all the hearts that couldn't be mended.
Voles and rabbits nested in her eaves. I remember

the alto of her voice, soft as the soughing of wind
in winter branches: plant-whisperer, wisdom-carrier,

peace-maker, strife-snatcher, husband-soother,
bone-house cancer-bearer, keeper of secrets, teller of lies.

Physick

She has no cure for this, though I summon her
from my head with her old wives' tales and remedies.

The clay-and-linseed poultice, daubed thickly
onto lint, warmed against a boiling kettle to draw

the pus away. Milkweed for warts, mustard wraps
to calm a chesty cough, styes roundly cursed with gold.

She'd bathe my graze of knees, apply a salve
of chamomile, soothe smarting flesh with aloe.

Once, hers were the hands that slapped a baby
into life, or eased the grief of sudden passing.

Now, in these uncertain times, would she unlock
the physick of herself, ladle out chicken soup and garlic,

brew potions on the stove to stop a fever? And though
she couldn't fix herself, or halt the rapid spread

from breast to bone, I take her ancient alchemy,
bind memory up in yew and thyme, ask for

a forgiving-charm, to heal the guilt of loving her
not well enough to take away the pain.

Wilt

The wind is lippy, inflates the sails of trees,
drowns out the sound of bees with his querulous tones.

Sun oven-dries the honesty, kindles withering
roses which have stayed too long without water;

petals languish in their scorch, a scatter
of pale pink fondant. Fireblight has killed

the apple-tree, honey-fungus the lilac. We erode
together in this dieback; the rings in my skin tell

a story of age, brown patches spread like canker.
My body has weathered storms and creeping spores,

is ready now for burning, but today I'm waiting
for this rain, which boasts of oceans, spins yarns

of shipwreck, horizons not yet dreamed of, says
that falling off the world is harder than it seems.

Urban Fox

Skinny dog-fox, hungered to his bones,
scrap-merchant and wheeler-dealer
of other people's trash; and in this hot reek
of city, where there's no dark, no silence,
he's sketched on the dusk, russet traced
over neon, a drawing so delicately done
that he's almost not-there, a trick of streetlight
and rain. His bark is a stalled engine, his scream
the echo of a passing siren; his eyes gleam
headlamps of yellow. But when he keens
for the forest, how it catches in your throat;
like the memory of a painting, or the wild
in us, lost somewhere out of the frame.

Brown Rat Mother Speaks

I made a man-trap out of chicken wire,
baited it with beer and chocolate cake
laced with the strongest poison I could find.

You are vermin to my species, litter
our runs with the dump of your lives,
teach your offspring to be scared of mine;

our cities are infested; plague-bringer,
sewage-dweller, swamp-swimmer, flea-enticer,
bore-tooth, corpse-eater, double-crosser.

I worry, worry, always driven; where's
the next meal to come from? Will my young
ones be safe? A mother's work is never done.

You make cartoons of my cousin mouse,
but I'm as cute as him. Watch how daintily
I eat, how my scurrying heart beats just the same.

Once, I saw a man gaze into a mirror,
as if pleased at what he saw. We have
no need of vanity to ensure our survival:

game-hunter, tree-destroyer, earth-polluter,
bird-shooter, deer-culler, garbage-maker,
badger-baiter, gold-hoarder, couch-potato.

Did you know that I grieve like a human?
Did you know that I dream of the future?

A Small Death

Lying at my feet, he reminded me of a vicar;
that black and white chasuble of feathers, an iridescent
sheen that might have been devotion shining through.

But vicars soar; through prayers, sermons, hymns,
they take off on a flight of ecstasy, divinity
in their fingers as they dish out consecrated wine,

break bread and summon the Host, remind us
of our past sins, those we have yet to commit,
the thoughtlessness and greed we fail to confess.

This little vicar's wings were broken, and though
I'd heard him preaching from the branches of the oak,
his voice was silent now. I laid him to rest

in a sanctuary of twigs and meadowsweet, his heaven
filled with blackbirds, the exultation of larks.

Constellations

This spring, a chain of satellites
is spawning through the evening sky,
a bright ellipsis circling the earth,

and here, a glut of tadpoles in the pond
strands of black Chantilly lace pleated
between the reeds and flowering rush.

Some already with a bud of legs,
but it will be weeks before new fingers
have learned to grasp the edge of a lily-pad

and haul themselves up to the sun.
They'll meet again, but never the same
as when they slipped from the silence

of their sealed globes; brief cluster
before that taste of freedom sent them
scattering like a broken string of pearls.

One day a constellation of eyes
will shine up from the surface. One day
they will bear the weight of worlds

on the green slope of their shoulders.
The blackbird hops small odysseys
from branch to branch, the planet

of his eye alert to worm and snail.
I see him land on the edge of the pond,
reach to pluck a dark pearl from the water.

Instructions for Light on Entering a Church Window

First, become a dragonfly, learn the art
of darting on a creed of stained-glass wings.

Enter the quiet sanctuary of glass. Bless
saint and martyr in their bright enamels,

sing psalm and hymn to primary colours
and praise all shades of cobalt and copper.

Preach light from dusty pulpits, and scatter
rosaries of gold through apse and chapel.

Make a chant from the lustre of yourself,
whisper a soft litany of rainbows,

and when you fade, know that in the ebbing
is held a weight of faith, reflected griefs,

confessions. Kneel in your dazzling habit.
Give absolution to the coming night.

Storm

What shall I do with this wind, which gusts
with unrelenting force, its voice
an open mouth chanting a mantra of howl?

How do I stop the trees from breaking
their spines on this gale, patch up split trunks,
and glue the branches back again?

Rosebay grows dizzy with the endless sway;
spider tangled in threads of silk spins
round and round, a whirling carousel.

Leaves are grimly clutching to twigs,
but the clouds have escaped, skitter off
like loose slates, hurl themselves at a horizon

that lowers with the hammer-blow of squall.
Acorns are a crack on window-panes,
like the snap of broken bones.

What shall I do with this wind, which makes
the upright horizontal, sweeps legs and feet
from the ground, singing in its shrouds?

I come to this weather with words burned
into me by August sun. Wind blusters away
the language of summer, leaves a hollow-out

like the empty oak on the crown of the hill
who speaks of his missing heartwood, threatens
to topple into himself, a blasted chimney.

I pocket this wind in my coat-of-many-colours.
Each seed a blowsy parachute, each seed an hour
that's flown, bringing me closer to the fractured dark.

Blackbeard lives under my bookcase

The sun is over the yardarm
                        and he's setting sail again
               from the corner where he hunches up,
bunches eight long legs
               like a ship becalmed,   a hulk
of stopped movement,   but desire to float
across the surface of the world grips him still;
              that swagger across the carpet,
                           not
sinking
              into its depths like a scuttled ketch
but a glide of his bulky keel.

I see him even in the dead of night; a sharper
                     pool of darkness
where he walks the plank of my eye.
        Nerves twitch in my throat as he pirates
insects from the air
              dances the hornpipe in front of me
knowing I will swoon
        as surely as a girl might faint
at the sight of Barbarossa.

He has no cutlass   but four of his eyes
are wearing a jaunty patch
      embellished with skull and crossbones.

I cry parley
                           but he's deaf to my pleas
and somewhere in his black heart,   this buccaneer
                   is afraid I'll cleave him to the brisket,
so he slips back to his mooring,
            weighs anchor,   weaves dreams
                                of looted treasure;
silk-wrapped cocoons of ants and beetles,
                    powdery scales of moth wings.

The Art of Constructing Birds

i. Rook

He's built for noise, burlesque.
So the voicebox should contain a swazzle
for squawking from the branches. His body
must be strong enough to resist
the knockabout of gales and blizzard,
be lustred as a midnight sun. Add
a squabble of feathers, baggy pantaloons.
Perched on his booth of oak, Mr Punch
pummels the feeders, claps his wings
like slapsticks, headbutts Baby squarely
in the mouth when it begs for worms and insects.
Applause is slow to come. But the leaves
begin to rustle, ask him for an encore,
the trees join in, give him a standing ovation.

Seagulls are easy. The blueprint is simple;
a folded origami of quills, an avaricious
disposition. Think clatter of dustbin lids,
the cry of a hungry kitten. Ice-cream muggers,
litter-lovers, they work the seafront in pairs,
their chatter a clickety-clack of fruit machines.
Make them out of paper, and they'll hurl
to the sky like a kite, whirl round and round
the thermals. You can watch for hours.
Paint the eyes as greedy as you like,
they'll always astonish. Add a bag of chips,
the remnants of a burger, you'll be
mobbed by friends for life. If you use
a strong enough glue, they'll last for years.

He comes as a DIY kit. Complete with chisel,
hammer, instructions for assembling. He'll
fluster the trunks, nail his colours to them,
play Knock-Down-Ginger on their doors.
At night you'll find him busy with home
improvements, adding extensions to the nest,
boring into the heartwood; an expert at
the bodge-job, Heath Robinson construction.
Trees shudder at his drumming, neighbours
complain at the noise. His mate is patient
as branches break beneath her, her name
carved into bark; she's seen it all before.
I imagine him drilling holes in the walls of heaven,
swathes of angels spilling like sawdust shavings.

Building A Drystone Wall

There's certainty to this work, a broth
of care and labour. Days of driving lanes
to spot a fallen wall, purloin its precious
spoil. Selecting shape and texture, feeling
the rock for faults. A trench, dug deep
and wide, earth levelled for foundations.
Then kneeling before it on the ground,
as though you'd slowly lowered from a pew.
The setting of them, layer on layer,
stacking blocks, a symmetry of line.
Fingers unused to wrestling landscape
are grazed and sore, plucked by this rough
psaltery of stone, and you hesitate, unsure
that diligence alone can keep the structure
whole. But your eye will show you
the right way, your hearting make it strong.

Making a Mammoth

after the Woolly Mammoth Revival Project

Scour the Arctic wastes until you find
a skeleton, unlocked from permafrost.
Extract the DNA, sequence the genomes.
Map an elephant's double-helix, stir
and mix it with the mammoth genes.
Add fat-cells, haemoglobin, shaggy fur.
Coil the tusks to perfect spirals, shrink
the flapping ears. Construct an embryo,
cherish it for two long years. And when
the calf slips from its caul, gently remove
the mucus, nestle him inside your arms.
Watch him as he wanders through the tundra,
this small chimera from a petri dish.
Teach him his heritage, how not to be extinct.

The Sea Learns Art

after Hokusai

Sea starts with simple scribbles, daubs
of foam. Abstracts from a saturated palette.

It hasn't learned to use a pen, draw fine lines
of demarcation, sprays the littoral with salt graffiti.

Later it discovers brush-strokes, how to balance
light and shade, moves on to finer work;

stipples of moonshine, white horses crafted
in spindrift, scrimshaws of bone on the shore.

Centuries on, it can etch a cave from a cliff,
carve the hardest boulder to perfect sculpture.

Its imagination grows. It dreams of exhibitions,
a showcase of water covering mountain peaks;

drowned cities, galleries of rip-tides, earth
scumbled in a wash of Prussian Blue.

See what it can do; how, like every artist,
it beats itself in frustration, flenses rock to sand,

reworks the coastline over and over, fearing
the ebb of talent. Its finest piece, a wave

suspended, curved for a fleeting moment.
Stillness was an art it never mastered.

The Museum of Past Culture

Exhibit 1: Woman from the Anthropocene

The Ugly Woman
on show in the museum
sits with folded hands.

Her mouth is downcast
as we file past her glass case;
part of the freak show

they have on display
showing how life used to be
in the bad old days.

No need to offend
the eye; body transplants will
change the plainest girl,

replace hair or face,
all blemishes smoothed away
by synthetic means.

The Ugly Woman
is made of wood and resin.
People point and laugh.

She cries to the moon.
The alchemy of its light
turns her into gold.

Just here, the Singing Tree.
Mechanical birds, of course;
real ones are now rare.

You can stand beneath
the metal branches, and hear
how dawn used to sound.

Pull this lever out;
a fledgling will appear by
magic from a branch.

Listen hard enough,
you'll find wingbeats can be heard.
As the evening falls,

the system will switch
over to murmurations.
Stay a little while,

marvel as the birds
whirl round in their formations.
The background music

is by Vivaldi,
played endlessly on a loop
for your enjoyment.

iii. Exhibit 3: Bone

Nothing much to see;
just the bowed arch of a spine
from a captured stag.

Here are the antlers,
velvet, his head of treasure.
He smells of heather,

lichen, tormentil,
of that soft leathery hide
once burnished to rust.

He came from the mist
with his coronet of tines,
as if he had sprung

from the forest's wings,
a mummer in a winter
masque, stepping into

footlights of shining
aconite, bold shoulders shawled
by a scut of cloud.

Hold his bones with care,
remember he was a god,
could leap to the stars

wander through the sky
in their ruts of trailing light.
Remember the chase,

the hard hunt of him,
how his eyes were always fixed
on this extinction.

Caring for Your A.I. Bees

Enclosed, your non-sting multi-rotor bees;
we hope they bring joy to your garden.

You may have problems with the default sound,
unless you've bought the Premium Wifi version;

due to a glitch in programming, the buzz
can sometimes change to an irritating whine –

if this continues, we strongly recommend
you remove the tiny speakers in their wings.

Clean your bees on a weekly basis, to keep
the circuit boards from clogging up with pollen.

Don't let them near a foxglove; it will swallow
them whole, deactivate the navigation.

Plant only annuals and cultivated shrubs,
spray wildflowers liberally with glyphosate

or your bees may start to get unruly, over-ride
the Hover App and swarm to nearby meadows.

Attach the plywood hive with the HD high-speed cable;
now you can watch them make synthetic honey,

and see the larvae hatch (if you've paid extra
to install our Adorable Website-Featured Baby Clones).

If there's a death, we're sorry for your loss; the bees
are connected to Google, and they'll already know.

Tomb Cats

They're huddled in this dark place, straight-jacketed
in linen, bodies filled with sand; the tight wrapped forms,

unaccustomed silence of their tongues, reminders
of those in old asylums, trapped in a sarcophagus of limbs.

Imagine the careful binding of ears and tails,
how paws were gently tucked inside the windings.

A farmer in another landscape carefully lifts a litter
of kittens from their nest of straw. Quick dunk in bucket,

their sacrifice not marked by oil and resin, the prayers
and rituals of priests, or small hearts kept in a canopic jar;

but here in the perfumed gloom, a surprise of mice,
perfectly packaged, waiting to be unloosed,

to be stalked among the chambers of the tomb,
their stored flesh welcome as an offering.

In 2019, more than 50 mummified cats, mice and falcons
were discovered in a 2,000-year-old tomb in Sohag, Egypt.

Cave-Bear

Lyakhovsky Islands, 2020

It wasn't love that woke him,
but the kiss from a dying sun.

In his hug of ice, he dreamed
of kingdoms blizzarded and cold

but permafrost has shrunk
from his hardened bones,

and in this peeling-back of land
he's risen from extinction

strung on a harp of weather
whose notes unlock his frozen ground.

He's flummoxed by this new age,
the heat, the smallness of things,

the stench of world in a nose
quickened after thirty thousand years.

He wakes to find his own kind famous,
stitched into softness, written into tales,

marvels that he, with his fierce snarl,
should calm the fears of children.

We stroke his miracle of fur, capture
him in photographs, study his DNA.

But he's come back emptied of himself,
a brittle box for which we've lost the key.

Sasha Restored

When they start to clean her up,
they're astonished to find she's
a luscious, film-star blonde.
Not handbag-leather grey like her
descendants, but a mass of gingery
curls; the undeveloped horns
are buds, small as retroussé noses.

No kid-glove treatment for this
starlet. Sasha strives for dignity
as she's hoisted onto a bench
where they rummage through
the intimacy of stomach for scraps
of a final meal, tease her slumped
remains to rhino-likeness.

She's a salvage job, cobbled back
together by art and science,
restored for the curious, who gawp
at this furry girl, want to take her
home to add to their stack
of shop-bought bears, felt dinosaurs,
the retail-hunters' trophies.

Sasha is silent, all femme fatale
and pouting. See her lumbering
through the tundra, flirting
with the mammoths, a sashay
of massive hips. Malingering in ice
for several thousand years, waiting
to be claimed by the paparazzi.

*In 2015 the first baby woolly rhino carcass was discovered
in Siberia. Named Sasha, it was later restored and put on
display in Moscow.*

The Mole Catcher

Slaughter must be done in comfort.
He straps the pads to arthritic knees,
eases the tension of the leather.

They'll give protection from the cold
as he kneels on sodden ground
among the tailings of earth and tiny stones.

Not many choose to be a mowdy-catcher;
a secret, solitary life. But it keeps him honest,
pays the rent, and he's proud of his profession,

the skill it takes to set a horsehair loop, fixed
with sticks of willow. He knows the turn
of weather, the ways of the land, can spot

a labour of moles from a hundred yards
away, pick out new mounds from old
by the colour of the soil, a practised eye.

There'll be money for him when he's hung
the bodies on a fence. Half-penny for each one,
and he'll sell the pelts to make a baccy pouch,

or a waistcoat for a gentleman with cash;
keep back a foot or two, flog them to farmers
at the market to ward off scrofula.

His fingers ache. He works the field from left
to right, mouth full of mumble-pins, flattens
the hillocks carefully as he hoists up every catch.

At night he dreams of burrowing, nose-first,
his broad hands splayed apart; feels the damp
of dark and loam, a touch of velvet on his skin.

Dodo

Thermals never soared me to the sky.
I was a Wallowbird, Turkey Cock and Knot-Arse,
waddling sluggard, round-rumped clumsy fool.

Not good enough to eat, too dense to fly,
a jester; with my cowl of a skull, a motley beak,
foolish yellow poulanes for my feet.

I went so swiftly, centuries passed before you saw
I was missing. No winners in this race. Just everyone
scrambling to stay alive, and not be dead as me.

A Visiting Pheasant Learns the Rules of Jousting

Present yourself in the brightest garniture.
Enter the lists, enclosed by mulberry hedge
and filled with beds of lupin and penstemon.

Preen your surcoat to burnished copper, swell
the wattle to angry red, push out the paunch
of a stomach to show that you mean business.

Sharpen your leg spurs for battle, polish
that lance of a tail. Do not be distracted
by sparrows; their dullness will bore you.

Run full-tilt at the enemy. Don't hesitate
or lower your beak. A glancing blow is enough
to chase a rook from a tasty morsel.

Flush out the biggest fat balls, raid the earth
for seed. Strut like a newly-dubbed knight
as he faces his first challenge.

The female whose favour you wear on your breast
will peck you gently, simper at your valour.
Treat her with chivalry. Win her feathered heart.

The Archbishop's Feast

after George Neville, 1465

He wanted peacock and curlew for this,
egret and seal, two hundred roasted cranes;
the subtlety, a dolphin baked in pastry.

The sky was cleared of birds. Bittern,
redshank, sparrow, all fell to net and bow,
pond emptied of teal, fields of their cattle.

So many wings and beating hearts to still,
a plethora of feathers to be plucked,
enough to fill a thousand noble beds.

What dreams he had of feasting! So vivid
he would wake in the middle of the night,
the taste of quail or plover on his tongue.

When he saw a heron rise from the river,
he thought of chestnut stuffing, pungent herbs,
felt the thin snap of bones between his teeth.

Here, gluttony was a virtue. He tore at thigh
and gizzard; crunched drumstick, crispy skin,
each course more lavish than the one before.

Afterwards, the piles of skeletons were
boiled for soup, discarded on the midden,
and he yearned for the texture of their flesh.

Heavy with fowl and ale, he nestled into
swansdown, his stomach full of birdsong.
Outside the air was silent, disembowelled.

Cloud-Whisperer

after Luke Howard, 1802

He named them because he could.
For the thrill of cirrus on his tongue,
cumulus and stratus a banquet
on the palate. Obsession ached
inside him, the need to claim
and classify. The logic of shape.

He envied their resolve,
the purpose that kept them feral,
wandering from place to place
like nomads, always heading
to the next clear patch of sky
that argued its blue emptiness.

Seeing them submerged in sea
or lake, he wanted to raise
them like a grounded swift,
throw them high as he could,
then call them back to his side
by the names that he had gifted.

Now I watch their floss and bustle,
like a woman hurrying to work
worries building inside her; ragged
fractus, weary with the day,
shapeshifting into mist, keeping
its nose to the grindstone.

Their bellies are full of storm
and fire, while mine has emptied
of passion. I think of the man who
organised the skies; how nothing
pleased him more than waking
to quilts of nimbus, cirrostratus.

Ghost Girls

Aberglasney, Carmarthenshire

To see this house is to love it. The intrigues
of knot-garden, parapet walk, where suitors'
pledges melt into air, elusive as fleeting ghosts.

Each morning, thirty hearths to clean.
Raking ashes from the grate, hands raw with dirt
and chilblains as we drew the dying embers back to life.

In winter, ice splintered in our footsteps,
cold clenched inside the stone, as we ran upstairs
with jugs of scalding water, or broke the surface

of the tub to wash the dirty linen. Until the day
we saw them; corpse candles floating
in the air, thin globes of bright blue flame.

They laid us on the bier, five of us in a row,
pale as white-skinned cattle; gave bread
and sixpence to the man who took our sins away.

Now I've shrugged off my flesh and my dust
collects in corners of these silent rooms. I miss
my shadow, that delicate fall of light behind me.

I am a blown moment, the faded haunt of gorse,
that closeness in the dark when you turn,
and something catches like a sudden breath.

Aberglasney is said to be haunted by the ghosts of five
maids, who died there overnight in the 1600s, possibly
from carbon monoxide poisoning from a charcoal stove

Peat Men

Cors Caron, Tregaron

They rise from the marsh, bog-smeared,
stinking of ale and a thousand years of peat.

Under the right moon, you'll see them
cut-and-come-again, dark burdens shouldering

the night, tongues slackened by loosestrife.
A place of wings and water, holding its ghosts

beneath spikes of asphodel and bedstraw,
a hustle of bees in rosebay, where cotton-grass

is buffeted to tufts of ribboned fleece,
and stars of butterwort fold gently over flesh.

Their sword was a spade, anger a red-hot spark
kindled each day inside a simple croft;

dirt covering the raw wound of their poverty,
the blistered hands that laboured long and hard

for this sullen-burning harvest. Men who sang
of ash, and lodged their hearts in earth,

dug futures from the mire, where one day
they'd be buried, pleached to roots of alder.

The Drowned

Only cathedrals drown magnificently,
go down with a clamour of bell and steeple,

chime from sunken tombs, swallowed by
reservoir or ocean. Villages just return to the roots

that made them, voices silenced by a wrongness
of water, their windows flapping like trapped fish,

doors jammed and swollen. There is a rot here,
of book and wooden floor, chimney, casement,

a rubble of flooded lives; tree and bush washed
out of life, plants deflowered in their watery beds.

Sometimes they rise again, these lost kingdoms,
showing littered broken stones, forests

of ruined stumps in the shrinking back of tides.
Perhaps names had been carved into trunks,

scrawled on wallpaper; pictures drawn in chalk
by children who once played along these streets.

Now the drowned are bubbling up, floating through
our throats. Listen to the thousand angry tongues.

Why grief is like being embalmed

because the bees' vibration is a small drill
boring into my skull

because even with my eyes glued shut
you are everywhere I look

because I'm both dead and alive
preserved in a sorrow of bones

because I reach for you, but find my fingers
cold as three thousand years of stone

because my face has stiffened to a mask
that passes for a smile

because I wear my skin as though I'm still
inside it, though each grain of pollen hurts

because my heart has been replaced
by a weight of granite

because I'm wrapped so tightly in this grief
that I'm bound to an afterlife of tears

because without you, my body is
a sarcophagus that can't be opened

because forget-me-nots lean towards the pond
as though to catch a whisper from the shallows;

two frogs are praying at the water's edge –
sun whets its knife along the slabs of shadow

Solastalgia

when the mountain walked away / sulked off in its enormous bulk / I thought it would be back / begging forgiveness / scree pouring down its face / saying it wouldn't happen again / those rages / the shove of boulders / tumbling with the force / my cheek red where a crag had slapped me / hard on the bone / bruises the colour of heather / but mountains will be mountains / you can't make them change unless they want to / and it was truly sorry, knows it has faults / though the therapist had gazed / deep into its flinty soul / found caves of melting stalactites / salty as tears / there was hope she said / some warmth lingering in the stone / if only it would stop / the soft tipple of streams down its throat / tipping liquid into its fells / foothills stumbling over themselves / waking with a hell of an overhang / but another shower and it was off / drinking in the soak of rain / taste of fermented clouds / until it was high as a kite, a soaring buzzard / off its peak on lush greens / new growth firing its temper / it was quick to anger in those days / some memory of lava heating its core / and it told me things would be different now / there would be flowers / tormentil and sundew / bees sipping among shrubs / sheep grazing in cotton-wool flocks / it was calm not like a million years ago / first flame then ice / but like all mountains / it was lying / packed its bags and went / I was left with an empty landscape / and a hole in my life / though I knew it was for the best / I grieved at the way it disappeared / without saying goodbye / and even though a city took its place / gave me everything I wanted / couldn't do enough for me / still at night I stare through the window / hope to hear the lurch of rock / climb its slopes / lie in corries again / not mind when an avalanche / hits me like a fist

The Vanishing Room

First it was a rabble of bees that swarmed inside
and vanished. That old magicians' trick,
art of smoke and mirrors and sleight-of-hand.

Next, a herd of elephants came hurtling
up the stairs. Pods of whales and dolphins,
leatherback turtles, rhinos. Schrödinger's cat.

The windows in this house are boarded up;
a place the lost sneak into chinks,
childhood clings on by its fingertips.

Nowhere to hide, though there's a hole
where once I hurled a cup, wide enough to let
a starling through, squeezed flat as a fallen leaf.

The chest of drawers has long since gone,
wardrobe dumped in a skip. Blinds have swallowed
nightmares, but keep their secrets well.

The door still has a hook for her towelling gown;
there are imprints where the dressing-table stood,
extinct as the bristles in her silver brushes.

Air is dusty from blankets, fluffed-up duvets;
and here my father also disappeared,
walls of memory dissolved, his landscapes blank,

while a past that didn't know it was endangered
hung like a light from the ceiling-rose,
tried in vain to banish the lingering shadows.

Now penguins pile inside, a sloth of polar bears,
padding softly across the faded carpet.
Their absence colds the room.

If the house grew fat with creatures, it never
complained. It was only when I searched for myself,
that I found my kind had vanished too.

The Grief Machine

whirrs away in the corner of the room,
turns itself on and off at random,
shape-shifts to many different forms.
To access it, you must download the app,
set guidelines for your level of distress –
a start and end date at the very least.

I've been caught too long in its churning
mechanical innards, as it replays my dreams,
hurls memories out like a trebuchet
into the slow fade of evening, where skeletons
of last light lurk in shadows, and day
redacts itself to one small gleam of sun.

The Grief Machine is a prayer, a wanting,
divides the wakeful night like a Book of Hours.
It scents the air with lavender and rue,
leaves me bouquets of love-lies-bleeding,
strews self-heal on my bed; in summer
brings carnations, a consolation of poppies.

The Grief Machine is rusty from tears; says
it knows exactly how I feel, talks me through
the Seven Stages. I've barely got past
Shock & Denial, a jumble of cogs and wheels
trundling round in circles. It won't fit in the skip.
A Grief Machine, remember, is for life.

The Revenant House

Damp had got through its abandoned shell,
trapped there like a man inside a whale
who doesn't know he's drowning.

It smelled of cigarette smoke still,
which even after all these years
clung to the life-raft of rotting woodwork.

I tried to navigate the memories; her
smiling, a basket of laundry in her arms,
him snoring quietly in the fireside chair.

The garden rambled away to itself;
with nobody to fight against, it had slipped
into senility of grass and climbing bramble.

Unmoored, I looked for an anchor.
There in the corner of the living-room,
which slumped inside its wet musk scent,

a scribbled pen-mark on the wall, made by
a child who once lived here, and had returned
to trawl for an unwillingness of ghosts.

A Recipe for Rewilding

Remove a human from his usual place.
Trim off the fatty trappings of his life,

so he is lean and raw inside his skin,
his mind unfixed and gently clarified.

Take his body's continents, season them
with sea-salt and the tang of lemon grass.

Turf his feet with thyme and fescue,
show them how to run in morning dew,

know their way along the ancient paths.
Take his hands and teach them to tender,

place a cup of longing in his palms.
Marinate his thoughts in a steep of kindness,

feed the old words back inside his mouth;
knead his heart until it beats to the sound

of a heron gliding from the marsh.
Taste him then, let him slip down your throat,

cool as a stream, as mountain air.
Feel the world rewilded on his tongue.

Kathy Miles - Biography

Born in Liverpool, Kathy lives near Aberaeron in West Wales. Her publications include *Bone House* (Indigo Dreams, 2020), *Inside the Animal House* (Rack Press, 2018), *Gardening With Deer* (Cinnamon Press, 2016) and *The Shadow House* (Cinnamon Press, 2009).

Kathy is a previous winner of the Bridport Prize, as well as the Welsh Poetry, Second Light, Wells Festival and Shepton Mallet poetry competitions. She has an MA in Creative Writing from the University of Wales, Trinity Saint David, and is a regular tutor on the Dylan Thomas Summer School. Kathy lives in a wooden self-build eco-house, and is passionate about gardening and helping to conserve the rivers and wildlife of her local area.

Palewell Press

Palewell Press is an independent publisher handling
poetry, fiction and non-fiction with a focus on books that
foster Justice, Equality and Sustainability.

The Editor can be reached on
enquiries@palewellpress.co.uk

9 781911 587835